# DALÍ:

## In Verse

AF472195

Sarah Hobbs

Foreword by Paul Chimera
~ Dalí Historian, Dalí Society ~

First published 2018 by Sarah Hobbs Poetry
**sarahhobbspoetry@gmail.com**

ISBN: 978-0-9567274-4-2

 A CIP catalogue record for this book is available from the British Library.

Print and bound by CreateSpace 4900 Lacross Rd, North Charleston, SC 29406, USA.

3 4 7 3 0 8 4

Distributed by Amazon UK, 60 Holborn Viaduct, London EC1A 2FD.



Visit **www.sarahhobbspoetry.co.uk** to read more about books, poetry, events and blog articles regarding poetry – and you can sign-up for e-newsletters so that you are always the first to hear of new releases.

*For poetry lovers and Dalí lovers alike:*
*born are kindred spirits of*
*culture and art.*

***

*"Those who do not want to*
*imitate anything, produce nothing."*
*~ Salvador Dalí ~*

***Previous works by this author:***

***Collections:***

*The Things That I Love*

*Sonnets Throughout A Year*

*Love Is Where The Heart Is*

***DALÍ: In Verse***

***Chapbooks:***

*Two Hills*

# Contents

# Preface

First and foremost, this is not an art book. It's not a book that tries to depict reasoning and rationale behind each masterpiece created by the great Salvador Dalí.

No. Instead this book is for me to add my interpretation to these masterpieces in a poetical response to his works.

***

Salvador Dalí was born on the 11$^{th}$ of May 1904 in Catalonia, Spain. He saw two world wars and a civil war during his lifetime.

Due to a tragic family incident when he was young, with the death of his older brother, Dalí's psychological issues started manifesting themselves from a young age.

More information regarding Dalí's early life can be derived from his autobiography, *The Secret Life of Salvador*

*Dalí.* This provides context and understanding to his thought processes and what eventually led to his artistic genius.

At the age of twelve he went to drawing school and while on summer vacation in Cadiques he was introduced to the style of modern painting by local artist Ramon Pichot. His first exhibition was held just three years later at the Municipal Theatre in Figueres, when he was just fifteen.

His work predominantly centred on paintings; however, he was also influential in the cultural forms of sculpture and film. This can be seen in the two videos, *Un Chien Andalou* and *L'Age D'Or*; and an example of his sculpting work can be seen with the *Lobster Telephone.* A full list of Dalí's surrealist works can be found at the back of this book.

Dalí led an eventful life and met some renowned individuals – not just from the art world; including Sigmund Freud, Pablo Picasso, Luis Buñuel, Alfred Hitchcock & Walt Disney, to name a few. He collaborated with these individuals on many occasions.

Throughout his time amongst the Surrealists he often debated vehemently with the movements founder Andre Breton, regarding the direction and stance that the movement was taking.

The pieces that Dalí produced over the years were enhanced by and took on imagery of a 'dream-like' nature; this allowed him to cover a multitude of topics within his works – no matter how far-fetched they may seem.

However, his influences for his art came from a variety of backgrounds; for instance, he tackled – even unconsciously – issues around war, religion and science. During the second half of his career physics, and most importantly, metaphysics played a huge part in the direction his work was taking.

He was aided in his works by the love of his life Gala – former wife of fellow surrealist Paul Éluard. They were married in 1934 in a civil ceremony. Gala was Dalí's muse and appeared in a number of his paintings.

Salvador Dalí died of a heart attack in his hometown of Figueres in 1989, aged 84.

Even after his death his legendary legacy lives on.

***

At fifteen I went on a school trip to London's Tate Modern Art Museum – that was the first time I encountered a Dalí masterpiece in real life. I loved it.

For two years, as part of my GNVQ Art & Design course, I looked at a number of his creations and spent copious amounts of time recreating them in colouring pencil.

To this very day, I find Dalí's works enthralling and I am constantly looking at them anew every time I see them.

Creatively Dalí opened my mind to imagination, which has now developed into my own works, even though I still pick up a pencil from time to time, it's usually the pen where my best work is done, hence the creation of this collection of poetry.

***

For me, this book is a kind of homage to one of the greatest artists and creative visionaries this world has ever seen. I have taken the titles from a careful selection of Dalí's works and have put together poems in response to them.

Symbolism and poetical devices such as metaphors, similes and alliteration, among others, are techniques that I seldom use; however these have been utilised within this collection to bring to light the surrealist nature of Dalí's works.

One thing to note is that this book encompasses a very small selection of Dalí's surrealist works – this is a personal selection of paintings that resonated deeply within me.

Please, enjoy this collection; I hope each piece written is as profound to you as its painted counterpart has been to me.

Open your artistic mind to the world of Dalí...

# Foreword

The poet, like the Surrealist, deals in imagination. In symbolism. In illusion and allusion; allegory and metaphor; simile and destiny. I cannot think of two things that pair so well as the verse of a great poet and the works of a genius artist.

**Dalí in Verse** doesn't merely comment on what is seen. It lifts up the skin of the paintings to which the author pays homage – laying bare a deeper meaning, and sharing with the reader how a painting by Dalí makes one feel, drilled down to the marrow. Dormant goose bumps, beware!

This poetry sees beyond the obvious.

Robert Frost wrote, "I have never started a poem yet whose end I knew. Writing a poem is discovering." Poet Sarah Hobbs has clearly discovered the immense emotional tsunami that a painting by Salvador Dalí is capable of creating.

Hobbs gets it.

Her poems share the DNA of Dalí, in a sense, because so much of the emotion Dalí intended us to experience through his extraordinary pictures Hobbs has captured and revealed in her insightful, skillfully written verse.

As a Dalí historian who had the privilege and joy of meeting the celebrated painter, and who has spent his entire adult life studying and writing about the life and work of the Catalan master, I know when someone is just going through the motions, and when he or she is truly in tune with the complexity and mystery of the great Spanish artist, the great "Divine" Dalí.

Sarah Hobbs is the latter. Her words drip – perhaps not unlike a melting watch – with honesty, astuteness, melancholy, joy, vision, and candor. As I said, she gets it.

We read, for example, in reference to Dalí's "Burning Giraffe," the poignant lines: "Orange flames rise high/as I employ to find/me still standing tall –/ proud and resigned/ to the fate that is/ my eventual demise."

The inexorable melancholy that is often the poet's mistress and muse informs her verse about Dalí's remarkable painting, "The Face of War," in which she writes, "Anguish, pain and misery upon their faces – their light and hope fading into nothingness." A glance at an image of this 1941 canvas instantly ratifies the power and rectitude of Hobbs' words.

Of course, there is plenty of sheer beauty in ***Dalí in Verse***, too. Of Salvador Dalí's iconic religious masterpiece, "The Sacrament of the Last Supper," Hobbs paints a hauntingly lovely word picture: "Now, I am married – / to my Father above. / The meal ends – heads bowed, / as I transcend to destiny...".

And she adopts an almost journalistically observational tone when, in writing about Dalí's great picture, "Geopoliticus Child Watching the Birth of the New Man," she reports "The fragile form of this planet / now forced to modify itself / entwined in political debate."

There is so much more within these sensitively chosen words of an accomplished writer. Poet Hobbs cleverly repeats stanzas that echo the repetition of images in Dalí's "Paranoia."

She artfully sculpts the very morphology of her text to accord with the unique nature of certain Dalí paintings: the words form a cross when she ruminates about "Christ of St. John of the Cross." They become cubes for Dalí's "Corpus Hypercubus." And a female form rises from the printed text when the subject turns to the painter's "Woman with Head of Roses."

Transcending it all, in my view, is the vision and soul that bubbles up in Hobbs' verse like the inspirational dreams that boil over in Dalí's art. The poet's affinity for the energy and the enigma that was Dalí is readily apparent. She has managed to let us feel what she feels. We're not merely casual observers; we're participants in the special experience of connecting at a visceral and spiritual level with the ineffable genius of Salvador Dalí.

It is a sure bet that Sarah Hobbs has long taken seriously the advice of e.e. cummings: "Well, write poetry, for God's sake, it's the only thing that matters."

Paul Chimera[1]
*~ Salvador Dalí Historian, The Salvador Dalí Society, Inc. ~*

[1] Paul Chimera is the author of the book, *Dali & His Doctor: The Surreal Friendship Between Salvador Dali and Dr. Edmund Klein.*

## THE BASKET OF BREAD

Cradled and swaddled
like a baby napping;
it sleeps in silence.

Yeast filled dreams,
doughy and malleable –
but still misshapen.

Cracks form on the crust.
Broken not torn,
revealing its innards.

Growls from snores
form as it is served
torn from its essence

being ripped from
the darkened womb
into the bright light of

the virginal tablecloth.

## THE PERSISTENCE OF MEMORY

Time comes back
it haunts us –
it daunts us,
with memories.

Memories deemed lost
they return
they yearn
for our remembrance.

Hands ticked
long and short
in newfound thought
as one is played

again and again.
Shiny and golden –
now I am beholden
by the hands of time.

While this memory, plays on repeat…

# THE GREAT MASTURBATOR

Self-pleasure comes in waves
again and again it engraves

our memory of endless lust
not of a body, physique or bust,

but of one's self and its desire
to explore itself and stoke the fire –

of what yearns within the soul
skin tingling and starts to crawl.

Movements becoming frantic –
employing subconscious tactics,

as wave after wave crashes upon
the gentle hands of everyone.

Self-pleasure coming in waves.

## THE ELEPHANTS

Mirrored
on stilts,
standing tall –
facing off.

Two sides
opposing
decisions
of the other.

Nothing
in the far
distance
but hills.

Realisation
that they
are actually
one and the same.

Elephants
with tusks,
greying
and imposing.

# THE BURNING GIRAFFE

## *i.*

Ablaze in the shadows
lost in the background.

Darkness ensues
and covers the ground.

Unnoticed and lost
in a world now blind.

Orange flames rise high
as I employ to find

me still standing tall –
proud and resigned

to the fate that is
my eventual demise.

My cries and tears are
stinging blurry eyes.

My body suddenly falls;
my soul gracefully flies.

## *ii.*

Back pain
soars through
my hips to my brain.

I'm being
pulled roughly
backwards in an arch.

My head
twisting in
profound agony.

Suffering
and becoming
distorted in darkness.

I am empty
the drawers of my
being have been opened

and my innards
have been revealed
to everyone. Secrets not safe.

Oblivious,
I have become,
to everything around me.

That a
burning giraffe
escapes my attention

smoldering in the darkness.

## CHRIST OF ST JOHN OF THE CROSS

Hanging.
Left arm.
Right arm;
suspended
limply, as
head falls
looking down upon the masses. Unassuming – humbled.
Regal in its posture. Pain coursing through thin tiny veins,
pumping the judgement of the many, as darkness takes
its hold
upon the
individual.
Feet are
together
bound by
the gravity
and the
weight
of the
world.
All of
this on
a single
person. As the
clouds form above;
calling - singing for Him
to come home. No more pain.
No more suffering. Not for Him – and
definitely not for the individuals oblivious below.

# CRUCIFIXION (CORPUS HYPERCUBUS)

Squared and rectangular you're cubed but hung taut and confused. Tears begin to sting my anguished eyes, as I gaze upon you struggling and

suffering in your bare nakedness. It hurts just seeing you – not imagining what pain you are going through – pinned up on your

static wooden frame. I glance once again, my watery eyes calling your name. But it makes no difference, the end is in sight, as darkness slowly

replaces the light. Your suffering ending – peace gradually descending as you begin your ascent to a greater plane of existence – where death

has lost its vicious sting. Instead, what is seen is your new beginning, a resurrection with the Father of Creation. Free – in peace – laying at rest.

## SOFT CONSTRUCTION WITH BOILED BEANS: PREMONITION OF CIVIL WAR

Disjointed and torn: yet to feel whole.
Gradually pieces methodically fit together.

Side-by-side revealing its naked form,
as the one entity struggles with itself.

Head detached as feet stomp on buttocks –
a strong arm pulls at a single breast.

Fighting is inevitable as pieces are pulling
themselves apart instead of together.

Chaos ensues until the resolution of
self-togetherness becomes apparent.

## SWANS REFLECTING ELEPHANTS

Sleek and graceful
the length of its neck stretches
to the water beneath –
whitish-grey poised in posture
whilst taking a drink of water.

Whilst taking a drink of water
whitish-grey poised in posture,
to the water beneath –
the length of its trunk stretches
sleek and graceful.

## METAMORPHASIS OF NARCISSUS

Is this my hand I see before me?
Floating from a pool – enigmatically;
but wait it's different – distorted.

Discoloured and misshapen
from what I see when I look down.
It does not feel like me at all,

but I cannot help but stare at it, as others
go on blindly living everyday lives –
bursting with unfulfilled satisfaction.

The water is muddied, trodden
by the wretched feet of difference –
watered footprints echoing across the sand,

as each foot walks through my thoughts,
while I ponder about the image before me –
reflecting and shimmering

the change – in me.

# THE FACE OF WAR

Their faces are etched and sewn into
the fabric of its darkened diseased skin.

Their names forgotten and lost to
the all-consuming darkness within –

the monster, the beast that is found
has been rudely awakened;

dulling away the brightened sound;
of the living, being securely fastened.

Hair shaved away – leaving it bare
as it observes the conquered around.

The question being asked, *"how is this fair?"*
As death seeps through war-torn ground.

Alas, blind ignorance to the warnings
of past events that cruelly devastated

the world before, leaving it yearning
for life and peace to be demonstrated.

Instead the cloud of death creeps slowly
and covers everything it sees and traces,

from people on high, to the very lowly,
anguish, pain and misery upon their faces –

their light and hope fading into nothingness.

## TWO PIECES OF BREAD EXPRESSING THE SENTIMENT OF LOVE

Torn in two
ripped apart
a trail of crumbs
shows the direction
that they are travelling.

Walking side-by-side
along a sandy path
shuffling together
as piece by piece
merging as one.

# DREAM CAUSED BY THE FLIGHT OF A BEE AROUND A POMEGRANATE

Eyes closed – colours form.
A pomegranate vortex appears
out of nowhere within icy-blue sky.

Tigers pounce paw first
out of its pipped core –
teeth bared, claws extended.

A fish attacks gum-first
wrapping its salty lips
tail first, as the tigers' roar booms.

Naked, a woman bathes,
as unknowing danger approaches –
barrel pointed and poised.

Striding along the horizon
an elephant towers high
over the waves – on stilted legs.

A bee flies noisily around
a blood-red pomegranate,
signalling the end of her vision.

I awake abruptly – the dream ends.

## THE MEDITATIVE ROSE

Stemless.
Reflective.
Surrounded
by quietness.

Petals opening
revealing its
core beneath –
fragile but honest.

Memories form
and come together:
emotions slowly rise,
as a single tear

forms on the
surface of a
lipped red petal
as it slowly falls

into meditative contemplation…

# THE HALLUCINOGENIC TOREADOR

Stomp!
    Vibrant colours form.

Stomp!
    Taking a bodily shape.

Stomp!
    It's enticed by my red flag.

Stomp!
    Numerously multiplying itself.

Stomp!
    It charges full of determination.

Stomp!
    I subtly side step out of the way.

Stomp!
    It crashes to the floor –
                                        and so do I.

# MOUNTAIN LAKE

Shiny. Shimmering.
Water glistens as
an eerie quietness descends.

Still. Silent.
In the distance a ringing
reverberates across the hills.

Alone. Arbitrary.
Bleakness of a voice
steeling itself to reveal all.

Hoarse. Harsh.
Deep and crackling
down the line, "Hello..."

Disguised. Desolate.
Crackle, crackling –
follows a loud deafening dial tone.

## WOMAN WITH A HEAD OF ROSES

My
head – full to the brim
with floral scents and
left to their own flowery and
natural conclusions. Filled
to bursting with images
of bees that fly
around
its
s
t
e
m
–
a
w
a
i
t
i
n
g
the slow and gradual process of pollination.

## THE TEMPTATION OF ST ANTHONY

Dark clouds swam like locusts
blacking out what is left of day.

I look down and I am naked.
Naked in body and bare in spirit.

Shapes begin to form from the
sun and the clouds above –

darkish greys and virginal whites
morph into monstrous animals

descending upon me with hooves
of judgement and righteousness.

On my knees, cross bared
my innocence is protested

vehemently to the Almighty's aide;
watching in professional astuteness.

Sun shines around these beings
passing out my just verdict.

## FORGOTTEN HORIZON

I can't for the life of me
remember what is beyond
that line I see before.

Its mystery entices me –
encouraging gently to
go forth and explore.

Curiosity engulfs me,
as spikes form at its crest
just beyond the shore.

Excitement grabs me –
I dance, sand between toes,
waiting to discover more.

Longing becomes me,
but no, there's no escape,
only what is laid afore…

## THE DISINTEGRATION OF THE PERSISTENCE OF MEMORY

I have forgotten –
what needs to be remembered.

I have forgotten –
what time of day it is.

I have forgotten –
what it is like to remember.

I have forgotten –
my own name.

I have forgotten –
life and how to live.

I have forgotten –
you.

I have forgotten –
the relentlessness of...

...forgetful memory.

## GALATEA OF THE SPHERES

Each rounded frame heightens your virtue.

A variety of goodness shining through.

Each circle taking a piece of you with them.

Their movements serenading your presence.

Your beauty enhanced by the elements.

There is no other that can compare to thee;

For your love – is what sets me free.

# THE SACRAMENT OF THE LAST SUPPER

Cleansing my spiritual self
around a table of friends.

I baptize myself within the
seven vials of wine consumed.

My confirmation has been
ordained by the Almighty.

Anointed as the 'Son of God'
I sit and digest myself.

Paying penance for the
sins of the human race.

Now, I am married –
to my Father above.

The meal ends – heads bowed,
as I transcend to destiny...

# SPIDER OF THE EVENING

Night composes the production
created in wavering construction,
as shapes begin to merge elegantly
movement emerging eloquently.

Legs form into arms and arms into legs.
Faces become distorted – disfigured.

The cello plays its melodic song –
dancers move in a choral throng.
Angels observe in trepidation
lost in musical expectation.

Arms move forward and backwards;
repeating over and over again.

A white horse becomes the lead,
as it is fired from a cannon – freed.
Soaring to its unknown destination;
on impact echoes a fierce explosion.

Dramatic, final, concluding –
the encore of the evening's performance.

Night's final curtain slowly falls,
the crowd emptying from the stalls,
emptying from the shallow depths
out the door and down the steps.

Coldness, darkness, tiredness.
A taxi pulls over and we get in.

# GEOPOLITICUS CHILD WATCHING THE BIRTH OF THE NEW MAN

We have over populated our world
to the point of apocalypse;
self-destruction undeniable.

The fragile form of this planet
now forced to modify itself
entwined in political debate.

Discussions of the future –
but taking no definitive action;
our world left defenceless.

Resources are being depleted
so that we can live in luxury,
but at what destructive cost?

Change to the globe's climate is
more prevalent than ever before;
the cause is possessive greed.

Affecting our understanding
of the world in which we live,
as it becomes unpredictable.

A new birth is much needed –
a delivery of a new beginning,
where salvation offers hope.

I watch as you emerge from
your refreshed gestation – anew;
a bright future now beckons...

# THE FIRST DAY OF SPRING

Slowly. Gradually.
Movement commences gently,
as figures appear on the horizon;
signifying emergence from
hibernation.

Romantically. Lovingly.
Lovers stroll hand-in-hand
taking a slow thoughtless walk –
their shadows accompanying them
forward.

Energetically. Fearlessly.
Children start to be free
from the constraints of Winter;
playing their games
happily.

Poignantly. Powerfully.
A pedestal is self-constructed
emerging from my ambition.
My head and facial features
Displayed for all.

Artistically. Creatively.
I produce a self-portrait
and frame it in strong metal
showcasing my persona
confidently.

Contemplatively. Expectantly.
Looking along the long
and winding road ahead
that leads us joyously to
Summer.

# APPARITION OF FACE AND FRUIT DISH ON A BEACH

Waves and plates crash
upon the sandy shore.

Appearing angelically;
a face I had not seen before.

Eyes of clay white
and lips lost of all colour –

sandy cheeks flushed from
the sun's celestial power.

Legs frozen to the spot,
fear paralyzing movement.

Confusion takes hold;
trying to process the moment.

It smiles gently at me –
full of devout grace.

The table now altered;
my lunch lost without a trace...

## THE LUGUBRIOUS GAME

I cry rainbows –
made up of naked colours.

Head bowed –
seductive shapes appearing.

Urges unfulfilled,
frustratingly building…

…my shame
blindly holds out its hand,

as pride
stalks sullenly away from me.

# LIVING STILL LIFE

Frozen like a photograph.
Remnants of life scattered
haphazardly across the scene.

Waves become still.
    Falling plates hang.
        Birds caught in flight.
            Glasses tipped and poised.

Everything life offers
now forever stationary –
until someone presses Play.

# GIRL AT THE WINDOW

She looks out the open window
as the salty sea air fills her nostrils.
She sees the sun brightly glow,
as her arms rest on the windowsill.
The hills in the distance call to her
saying her name over and over again –
while grey clouds roll over the shore.
Entranced in place she does not stir.
Suddenly it starts to heavily rain
absorbed by the scene's melodic lure.

*In the form of an "English Ode'.*

# SLAVE MARKET WITH THE DISAPPEARING BUST OF VOLTAIRE

I hide in the shapes of consumers.
Browsing.
Furrowing.
Subjugating their impulses.

I linger in front of shadows
Poised.
Ready.
To make my thoughts known.

I am approached by sellers.
Pushy.
Assertive.
Negotiating their fees.

I try to persuade passersby.
Ardently.
Zealously.
Of their recent purchases.

I begin to slowly fade away.
Dwindling.
Vanishing.
Unsuccessful in my quest...

## PORTRAIT OF MY FATHER

Stern-faced poised and fixed –
rocking back-and-forth
sitting in a chair transfixed.

A twitch by the eye's tics
as he considers what's in store –
stern-faced poised and fixed.

Pipe in hand – tobacco mixed,
feet scuffing dust upon the floor;
sitting in a chair transfixed.

White shirt, nothing risked,
his tobacco tightly secured.
Stern-faced poised and fixed.

Greying hair, added to the list
of the aging man – I see before,
sitting in a chair transfixed.

A curl of his tight lips twist,
as he remembers a lost thought.
Stern-faced poised and fixed –
sitting in a chair transfixed.

# MORPHOLOGICAL ECHO'

A golden carpet is laid out
as the way is placed before
the sandy ramshackle town;
a local welcome bestowed.
Bestowed.
Bestowed.

Stone upon stone placed
methodically constructing
an entrance to a location
appearing gently; hospitable.
Hospitable.
Hospitable.

The horizon signals the
neighbours' picturesque
smaller village and sets
out the scene: tranquil.
Tranquil.
Tranquil.

Viewing the setting
of the dusty urban
surrounding buildings;
dark, desolate, destitute.
Destitute.
Destitute.

To the right, a flicker of
Heat-filled light appears
suddenly, out of nowhere;
smoke floats softly, signaling.
Signaling.
Signaling.

The structure of the
place fiercely ablaze
changed – transformed,
transposed, transfixed.
                Transfixed.
                              Transfixed.

                              Altered.
                Altered.
Altered in appearance.
Its meaning changed,
as its bodily exterior
has become reformed.

# APPARATUS AND HAND

The subconscious needs to be formed –
strong, sturdy and steel-like in foundation.

Piece-by-piece is delicately placed;
subtle, slight and slender in appearance,

but do not be fooled by its size, as it is
abled, accomplished and adept in fulfilling

each of their duties – masterfully.
Skilled, successful and smart in approach.

Imaginings and wonderings become
soldered, stuck and stiff in its rightful place.

Each playing their part of the narrative;
assured, assertive and approving in its form…

…desires construction now complete.

# MELTING WATCH

Hands with no fingers
point at both five and six at the same time.

Drip feeding
the obscure notion
that time has become
merged.

Blurred by the
thought
of being late
and running
out of time;

whilst not forgetting
meal times,
or bedtimes, or playtimes.

Social gatherings
now happen at the
start of the day.

Breakfast is
now served
prior to going to sleep.

Time – has lost all meaning!

## THE BATHER

Her toe rests upon
the sandy shore –
hair blowing in the
fresh sea breeze.

The rest of her
person can be seen
bobbing and dancing
along the horizon.

Lost in the moment
as wave after wave
crashes against the
rocks holding her still.

## THE HAND

Extended but empty of contents / nothingness offered in place / of normal contributions. / Masses of people gather / to see what has been brought / but hark, alas – this is not the case. / The hand that feeds us / now barren and sterile / dust in place of sustenance. / Anger and revolt shines through / the vast crowd now amassed / in front of the alter. / *"One morsel to touch our lips / quench our hunger / make us virile again."* / No response from those / who watch with / sated bellies and quenched thirsts. / People below left to / watch with hunger-filled eyes.

## GALATÉE

Sculpted in ice-white
        your form taking shape
each piece of you now
        being brought forward
into its physical and
        rightful position to find
your identity's beauty;
        natural – gracious. Your
movements dance on
        and on, bringing light to
the darkness that has
        become all consuming,
but you, yes, wonderful
        you, have found the light
that originated from the
        perfection of your marbled
construction…breathtaking.

## THE DREAM

Even here he halts my fantasies
blocking them from existence.
It recurs to me, every night,
my eyes closed – persistent.

Reaching deliriously vivid visions;
Alas they are shown no more.
Kept hidden and suppressed,
deep within my psychic core.

However, its remnants still lurk,
crawling and feeling their way
to the surface of my subconscious –
– feeling them gnawing at my brain.

I am lost. A slave to my inner
thoughts and what they show.
Images strategically pulled into
flashbacks – they come and go.

But their essence lives on and
inspires me to follow my desires,
to succumb to passions allure
my mind and heart in lusty fire...

...my awakening brings a new dawn.
One dark and not so sweet
as the one I left behind me is
where desire and the mind meet.

Reality shows itself to disallow
the passion that engulfs me.
Instead I am to find alternative
ways to fulfil my carnal needs.

Nothing will match the extent
of the images I have been shown –
now I am stunted, shortened;
not allowed to let my longing flow.

I see you in the flesh, but I see
that you are an imposter – unreal.
I try to comprehend my sight,
but I am confounded – it's too surreal.

...My subconscious bids me to sleep.
It calls me to lay my head down
and close my eyes tightly, so I
can return to lust's playground...

## SURREALIST ARCHITECTURE

Disfigured and disjointed in creation.
Held together by silver spoons,
tethered by their own handles,
unprovided and underprivileged.

Uncontrollable forces pulling
them together, obscured shapes
becoming one single entity:
merging into a metallic union.

Colours yet to show themselves;
hidden among the movement
of parts being assembled –
brought together piece-by-piece.

Fragmented stories become fused;
solidified in their sole narrative –
emptiness of the barren horizon
a quiet signal for a utopian future.

# ATAVISTIC VESTIGES AFTER THE RAIN

What was hidden, is now visible; in plain sight.
Revealed in its full beauty. The watery beads
drop down in full force washing all the dust from
our naked forms. The lines of our bodies revealing
the primal nature of human beings. How
their very history is shown in their blue/grey
veins, as each tiny droplet falls purposefully
on its target. I watch consumed with profound
amazement, as the world around me is exposed
in full glory. Bones tell the tales of lost remnants
of the past brought forward to the present.
Telling the stories of years and times lost to
the records of history. What is clear from
what is now made known is that we are what we
used to be. The present creates the future
and the future now becomes the past.

But as each drop enters the puddle below it
begins to disclose the very nature of not only us as
individuals, but of our very history and how it has led
us to where we are today and the direction the future takes.

## PARANONIA

She is on her pedestal.

She is on her pedestal –
awaiting confirmation.

She is on her pedestal –
awaiting confirmation
of her many thoughts.

She is on her pedestal –
awaiting confirmation
of her many thoughts;
talking to each other.

She is on her pedestal –
awaiting confirmation
of her many thoughts.
Talking to each other,
as each voice gets louder.

She is on her pedestal –
awaiting confirmation
of her many thoughts.
Talking to each other,
as each voice gets louder.
Screaming in unison.

She is on her pedestal –
awaiting confirmation
of her many thoughts.
Talking to each other,
as each voice gets louder.
Screaming in unison.
Until finally – quiet.

She is on her pedestal –
awaiting confirmation
of her many thoughts.
Talking to each other,
as each voice gets louder.
Screaming in unison.
Until finally – quiet;
Peace prevailing over noise.

# ARMCHAIR WITH LANDSCAPE PAINTED FOR GALA'S CHATEAU AT PUBOL

Gala,
When you sit and rest your legs
on this chair your head is filled
with imaginings of time spent
within the confined walls of your
castle. Tall and grey they shelter
us from prying eyes from the
outside. Inside it is just you
and me – together; like it
should be. Spending hours
passing the time; painting,
writing, talking, making love.
Being creative is who we are,
my dear Gala. It is our special
time; a time where we are
becoming one creative force.
This is our ideal holiday. We,
together, spend our time in
blissful tranquility. I must
leave you now, as is now our
custom, to yourself. However,
all I ask is occasionally you
take a moment now and then
to have a seat on your chair
of remembrance. It's all I ask.
Dalí

# AUTUMNAL CANNIBALISM

As Summer draws its end
a new beginning approaches;
grey in outlook and bleak
in its assured countenance.
Awaiting the arrival of
the darkness and the cold;
it reveals its plans for the end
of the penultimate season.
*Winter is coming* – for certain.

Grey in outlook and bleak
in its assured countenance.
Awaiting the arrival of
the darkness and the cold;
it reveals its plans for the end
of the penultimate season.
*Winter is coming* – for certain.

Awaiting the arrival of
the darkness and the cold;
it reveals its plans for the end
of the penultimate season.
*Winter is coming* – for certain.

Revealing its plans for the end
of the penultimate season.
*Winter is coming* – for certain.

*Winter is coming* – for certain.

# THE THREE AGES

## *i.*

## *Old Age*

Bones bowing. Mane mellowing.
Years taking their toll.

Measured movements. Speech slurred.
I think before doing.

Tangled thoughts. Muddled minds.
Struggling for answers.

Crooked column. Stumbling steps.
Cane supporting.

## *ii.*

## *Adolescence*

Towering above with an
assured posture
and a straightened spine –

Youthful exuberance
surrounds my aura;
striding with poise.

I survey my surroundings
confident, ambitious;
ready to take on the world.

## *iii.*

## *Infancy*

Arm, before leg.
I must remember –
arm, before leg.

Inch, by inch
my body moves;
inch, by inch.

Pull – not push.
Clawing – crawling.
Pull – not push.

## CELESTIAL CORONATION

I dance on the moon,
as stars shoot from
the roots of its craters.

My defining moment approaches;
I am dressed for it in full glory.

Meteor showers explode
above serenading my
entrance to celestial royalty.

My defining moment approaches;
I am dressed for it in full glory.

Protected by the glinting
armour supplied by
angels sent to guide me.

My defining moment approaches;
I am dressed for it in full glory.

Focusing and planning
the details of mine
and my lines spiritual reign.

My defining moment approaches;
I am dressed for it in full glory.

## DALÍ

You perceive shapes and objects –
form them into the narrative
that you explore within the
construction of your works of art.

Form them into the narrative,
the characters you have built –
construction of your works of art,
displaying your true persona.

The characters you have built
tell obscure surrealist stories;
displaying your true persona –
scenes depicting your true self.

Tell obscure surrealist stories
that you explore within the
scenes depicting your true self
you perceive shapes and objects.

"The fact that I myself, at the moment of painting, do not understand my own pictures, does not mean that these pictures have no meaning; on the contrary, their meaning is so profound, complex, coherent, and involuntary that it escapes the most simple analysis of logical intuition."

Dalí

# Afterword

Writing is what I love to do. Just as Dalí loved to paint. So, it seemed for me, the best way to show my appreciation for his art form is with mine.

I'm not saying this was an easy ride – far from it.

I had to go deep into the psyche and the history behind not only Dalí's painting but Dalí himself to effectively write this.

Dalí is a fascinating individual who for me exudes creativity, ingenuity and intelligence – an artist far ahead of his time.

The masterpieces that he came up with are so awe-inspiring that I could not help but to get creative in response to them.

He has been such a big part of my creative life that, for me, I would have felt unfulfilled if I had not done something to commemorate the effect he has had on me.

It was whilst on one of my many visits to the Tate Modern Art Gallery in London that creating this collection of poetry together.

Staring at a postcard with the painting 'Metamorphosis of Narcissus' printed on it I recalled the passion and the excitement I had when I was copying one of Dalí's pieces in coloring pencils at the age of 15 – and I wanted to note, then and there, how that piece made me feel.

Then it hit me – I could do this with other pieces of his. Thus, the creation of this collection of poetry was born.

As I mentioned earlier, writing this collection was not a walk in the park – in fact it was quite challenging. I wanted to give an accurate representation on each piece and how it made me feel and think.

I also came to realise that actually I did not know very much of Salvador Dalí, as a person. The extent of my knowledge was only of a small selection of his work and none of his influences and influencers. So, I began to read – and read I did.

His autobiography and a very informative professional biography by Dawn Ades helped me to understand him as a person and therefore provided a richer understanding of his work. I would highly recommend both books if you want to know more about Dalí – details of both are included within the 'References' section at the end of this book.

Whilst writing this collection I kept in mind the following quote by Dalí:

*"Have no fear of perfection – you'll never reach it."*

It helped me to understand that I wrote this as a personal account of how his work makes me think and feel and not an analytical and educational piece of work; therefore, it did not need to be refined to such a clinical standard.

I tried, within this collection, to include various visual and literary forms when writing each piece. I must admit, this challenged me, but I found that as I did this more and more it was flowing naturally and worked extremely well alongside the content of each poem.

This tested me in ways that I have never been tested before, so not only has this collection of verse helped me to grow in my love for Dalí and his work, but it has also helped me develop and extend my poetical abilities.

Anyway, I hope you enjoyed reading this, as much as I have writing it.

Sarah H

# Acknowledgments

Without Salvador Dalí I would not have had the influence and inspiration to write this collection of poetry, so I would like to posthumously thank him for his lifetime's contribution to the world of art and culture.

In this respect, I suppose I ought to also thank those who inspired him and his works, from; Dada, Raphael, Bronzino, Francisco de Zurbarán, Vermeer and Velázquez, to name a few. Thank you for providing Dalí with passion and inspiration to create his masterpieces.

The Dalí Society was instrumental in helping me to achieve the right legalities in finalising the publication of this book. A big, big thank you needs to go to Joseph Nuzzolo, Founder and President of the Society and Paul Chimera, Dalí Historian.

Dawn Ades' book 'Dalí' was a massive help in guiding me in not only his professional career, but his wider psychological outlook on topics he painted and the sociological impact on his thought processes. Thank you Dawn, your book truly helped me paint a clearer picture of who Salvador Dalí actually is.

Poet Inua Ellams' collection #AFTERHOURS was influential in inspiring the structure and approach to the writing of each piece within this book, as he paid homage to various poets by recreating some of their works with his words: so, a big shout out needs to go to Inua and his outstanding collection of verse. I am sure it will go onto inspire many more poets in the future.

Of course, I would not have been able to put this book together if it was not for the love and support of my wonderful partner, Kathleen, and the confidence she gives me every day to be my best and to better myself. Without her guidance and support this book would still just be a tiny *flicker* of an idea in my head.

Also, a big thank you must go to my good friend and Editor-In-Chief, Kathryn Hodge, who brings a sense of finality and order to the chaos; which is my writing. Massive thanks must also go to Nicholas Edwards for proofing my manuscript and keeping an eye-out for those pesky apostrophes. Thank you both so much for all your hard work in helping me put the finishing touches to this collection.

As always, I have to give a big shout out to my friend, supporter and mentor Benjamin Zephaniah, who always makes me strive for more and test myself with my writing. You are an inspiration in every aspect of my poetical life; thank you Benjamin.

Then there are you guys. Without your enthusiasm to read my work, my poems would come to nothing. They would be like whispers lost in a wind. So, thank you for taking the time to sit and read this collection. It means so much to me. You're all amazing.

# References

Ades, D. 1982. *Dalí (World of Art).* London, England: Thames & Hudson Ltd.

Atavistic, accessed on 26 February 2018, http://www.dictionary.com/browse/atavistic

Chimera, P. 2006. *Little Known Salvador Dalí Work Inspired by German Scientist*, The Salvador Dalí Society, accessed on 20 March 2018, http://www.Dalí.com/little-known-salvador-Dalí-work-inspired-german-scientist/

Dalí, S. et al., 1942. *The Secret Life of Salvador Dalí.* United States of America: Dover Publications.

Gala Dalí Castle in Púbol. History, accessed on 20 March 2018, https://www.salvador-Dalí.org/en/museums/gala-Dalí-castle-in-pubol/historia/

Galatea (mythology), accessed 29 November 2017, https://en.wikipedia.org/wiki/Galatea_(mythology)

Geopolitics, accessed 21 November 2017, https://en.wikipedia.org/wiki/Geopolitics

Homepage, Salvador Dalí, accessed 4 May 2017, http://www.salvadorDalí.com/

Lugubrious, accessed 2 January 2018, https://en.wiktionary.org/wiki/lugubrious

Morphological, accessed 3 January 2018, https://en.wikipedia.org/wiki/Morphology_(biology)

Narcissus (mythology), accessed 28 June 2017, https://en.wikipedia.org/wiki/Narcissus_(mythology)

Salvador Dalí, Wikipedia, accessed 2 May 2017, https://en.wikipedia.org/wiki/Salvador_Dalí

Salvador Dalí Quotes, Brainy Quote, accessed 3 May 2017, https://www.brainyquote.com/quotes/authors/s/salvador_Dalí.html

Temptation of Saint Anthony in visual arts, accessed 18 October 2017, https://en.wikipedia.org/wiki/Temptation_of_Saint_Anthony_in_visual_arts

Toreador, Wikipedia, accessed 15 September 2017, https://en.wikipedia.org/wiki/Torero

Vestige(s), accessed 26 February 2018, http://www.dictionary.com/browse/vestige

Voltaire, accessed 2 January 2018, https://en.wikipedia.org/wiki/Voltaire

WikiArt, Salvador Dalí – All Works, accessed 16 August 2017, https://www.wikiart.org/en/salvador-Dalí/all-works

# Painting Details

*Below is a list of images of the paintings mentioned within this book. Sizes are structured as follows:* cm × cm (in × in). Information on the paintings cited in this book was taken from Wikipedia and WikiArt.

**1.** *Basket of Bread*, c. 1926. Oil on canvas, 31.75 × 31.75 (12.5 × 12.5). Salvador Dalí Museum, Florida.
**2.** *The Persistence of Memory*, c. 1931. Oil on canvas, 24 × 33 (9.5 in × 13). Museum of Modern Art, New York City.
**3.** *The Great Masturbator*, c. 1929. Oil on canvas, 110 × 150 (43.3 × 59.1). Museo Nacional Centro de Arte Reina, Madrid.
**4.** *The Elephants*, c. 1948. Oil on canvas. Private collection.
**5.** *The Burning Giraffe*, c. 1937. Oil on panel, 35 cm × 27 cm (13.8 in × 10.6 in). Kunstmuseum, Basel.
**6.** *Christ of Saint John of the Cross*, c. 1951. Oil on canvas, 205 × 116 (80.7 × 45.67).

Kelvingrove Art Gallery and Museum, Glasgow.
**7.** *Crucifixion (Corpus Hypercubus)*, c. 1954. Oil on canvas, 194.3 × 123.8 (76.5 × 48.7). Metropolitan Museum of Art, New York City.
**8.** *Soft Construction with Boiled Beans (Premonition of Civil War)*, c. 1936. Oil on canvas, 100 × 99 (39 × 39). The Louise and Walter Arensberg Collection.
**9.** *Swans Reflecting Elephants*, c. 1937. Oil on canvas, 51 × 77 (20.08 × 30.31). Private collection.
**10.** *Metamorp hosis of Narcissus*, c. 1937. Oil on canvas, 51.2 × 78.1 (20.12 × 30.75). Tate Modern, London.
**11.** *The Face of War*, c. 1940. Oil on canvas, 64 × 79 (25.2 × 31.1). Museum Bojimans Van Beuningen, Rotterdam.
**12.** *Two Pieces of Bread Expressing the Sentiment of Love*, c. 1940. Oil on canvas, 51 × 40.5 (20 × 15.9). Dalí Theatre and Museum, Figueres, Spain.
**13.** *Dream Caused by the Flight of a Bee Around a Pomegranate a Second Before Awakening*, c. 1944. Oil on wood, 51 × 40.5 (20 × 15.9). Thyseen-Bornemisza Museum, Madrid.
**14.** *The Meditative Rose*, c. 1958. Oil om canvas, 36 × 28 (14.17 × 11.02). Huntsville.
**15.** *The Hallucinogeni c Toreador*, c. 1968-1970. Oil on canvas, 398.8 × 299.7 (157 × 118). Salvador Dalí

Museum, Florida.

**16.** *Mountain Lake*, c. 1938. Oil on canvas, 73 × 92.1 (28.74 × 36.26). Tate Modern, London.

**17.** *Woman with a Head of Roses*, c. 1935. Oil on wood panel, 27 × 35 (13.78 × 10.63). Kunsthaus Zürich, Zurich.

**18.** *The Temptation of St Anthony*, c. 1946. Oil on canvas, 119.5 × 89.7 (47.05 × 35.31). Royal Museums of Fine Arts of Belgium, Brussels.

**19.** *Forgotten Horizon*, c. 1936. Oil on wood, 22.2 × 26.7 (8.74 × 10.51). Tate Modern, London.

**20.** *The Disintegratio n of the Persistence of Memory*, c. 1952-1954. Oil on canvas, 25.4 × 33 (10 ×13). Salvador Dalí Museum, Florida.

**21.** *Galatea of the Spheres*, c. 1952. Oil on canvas, 65 × 54 (25.59 × 21.26). The Dalí Museum, Figueres, Spain.

**22.** *The Sacrament of the Last Supper*, c. 1955. Oil on canvas, 267 × 166.7 (105 × 65.6). National Gallery of Art, Washington DC.

**23.** *Spider of the Evening*, c. 1940. Oil on canvas, 40.5 × 50.8 (15.94 × 20). Salvador Dalí Museum, Florida.

**24.** *Geopolitic us Child Watching the Birth of the New Man*, c. 1943. Oil on canvas, 32 × 46 (12.5 × 18). Salvador Dalí Museum, Florida.

**25.** *The First Days of Spring*, c. 1929. Oil and collage on panel, 49.5 × 64 (19.5 × 25.2).

Salvador Dalí Museum, Florida.

**26.** *Apparition of Face and Fruit Dish on a Beach*, c. 1938. Oil on canvas, 114.8 × 143.8 (45.2 × 56.6). Wadsworth Atheneum, Connecticut.

**27.** *The Lugubrious Game*, c. 1929. Oil and collage on cardboard, 44.4 × 30.3 (17.5 × 11.9). Private collection.

**28.** *Living Still Life*, c. 1956. Oil on canvas, 125 × 160 (49.64 × 63.76). Salvador Dalí Museum, Florida.

**29.** *Girl at the Window*, c. 1925. Oil on paper, 105 × 74.5 (41.34 × 29.33). Museo Nacional Centro de Arte Reina, Madrid.

**30.** *Slave Market with the Disappearing Bust of Voltaire*, c. 1940. Oil on canvas, 47 × 66 (18.5 × 26). Salvador Dalí Museum, Florida.

**31.** *Portrait of My Father*, c. 1925. Oil on canvas, 1,045 × 1,045 (411 × 411). Museu Nacional d'Art de Catalunya, Barcelona.

**32.** *Morphological Echo*, c. 1934-1936. Oil on panel, 64 × 54 (25 × 21). Salvador Dalí Museum, Florida.

**33.** *Apparatus and Hand*, c. 1927. Oil on panel, 62 × 47.5 (24 × 18.7). Salvador Dalí Museum, Florida.

**34.** *Melting Watch*, c. 1954. Oil on canvas, 72 × 88 (28.35 × 34.65). Private collection.

**35.** *The Bather*, c. 1928. Oil, beach sand and sea shells on panel, XX × XX (20.5 × 28.25). Salvador Dalí Museum, Florida.

**36.** *The Hand*, c. 1928. Oil and collage on canvas, 41.28 × 66.04 (16.25 × 26). Salvador Dalí Museum, Florida.
**37.** *Galatée*, c. 1954. Oil on canvas, 100.6 × 101 (39.63 × 39.75). Private collection.
**38.** *The Dream*, c. 1931. Oil on canvas, 96 × 96 (37.80 × 37.80). Cleveland Museum of Art, Cleveland - Ohio.
**39.** *Surrealist Architecture*, c. 1932. Kunstmuseum Bern, Switzerland.
**40.** *Atavistic Vestiges After the Rain*, c. 1934. Oil on canvas, 52.07 × 62.23 (20.5 × 24.5). Private collection.
**41.** *Paranonia* , c. 1935-1936. Oil on canvas, 46 × 38 (18.11 × 14.96). Salvador Dalí Museum, Florida.
**42.** *Armchair With Landscape Painted For Gala's Chateau At Pubol,* c. 1974. Oil on canvas, 26 × 40 (10.24 × 15.75).
**43.** *Autumnal Cannibalism*, c. 1936. Oil on canvas, 65.1 × 65.1 (25.63 × 25.63). Tate Modern, London.
**44.** *The Three Ages*, c. 1940. Oil on canvas, 49.86 × 65.1 (19.63 × 25.63). Salvador Dalí Museum, Florida.
**45.** *Celestial Coronation*, c. 1951. Oil on canvas. Private collection.
**46.** *Dalí,* image of Salvador Dalí taken from, https://www.wikiart.org/en/salvador-Dalí on 19.06.2017.

# Full List of Dalí's Surrealist Works

*All of the works listed below are a mixture of surrealist paintings and sculptures of Salvador Dalí. This has come from WikiArt. Not all of these pieces have had a poem written about them and by the looks of it this book has only really scratched the surface...*

1. Portrait of Garcia Lorca, 1924
2. Coupes 6, 1925
3. Study for "Honey is Sweeter than Blood", 1926
4. Apparatus and Hand, 1927
5. Harlequin, 1927
6. Honey Is Sweeter Than Blood, 1927
7. Nude Woman in an Armchair, 1927
8. Big Thumb. Beach. Moon and Decaying Bird, 1928
9. Bird, 1928
10. Composition, 1928
11. Female Bather, 1928
12. Female Nude, 1928
13. Inaugural Gooseflesh, 1928
14. Little Cinders (Senicitas), 1928
15. Ocell. Peix, 1928
16. Shell, 1928
17. Soft Nude (Nude Watch), 1928
18. Sun, 1928
19. Symbiotic Woman-Animal, 1928
20. The Bather, 1928
21. The Ram (The Spectral Cow), 1928
22. The Rotting Bird, 1928
23. The Rotting Donkey, 1928
24. The Spectral Cow, 1928

25. Unsatisfied Desires, 1928
26. Un Chien Andalou (film still), 1928
27. Accommodations of Desire, 1929
28. Desecration Descripti, 1929
29. Illumined Pleasures, 1929
30. Imperial Monument of Woma-Child. Gala (Utopian Fantasy), 1929
31. Invisible Man (Study for the Painting), 1929
32. Playing in the Dark, 1929
33. Portrait of Paul Eluard, 1929
34. Profanation of the Host, 1929
35. Sometimes I Spit with Pleasure on the Portrait of my Mother (The Sacred Heart), 1929
36. The Ants, 1929
37. The Enigma of My Desire or My Mother, My Mother, My Mother, 1929
38. The First Days of Spring, 1929
39. The Great Masturbator, 1929
40. The Lugubrious Game, 1929
41. The Two Balconies, 1929
42. Chocolate, 1930
43. Invisible Sleeping Woman, Horse, Lion, 1930
44. Invisible Sleeping Woman, Horse, Lion, 1930
45. Paranoiac Woman-Horse (Invisible Sleeping Woman, Lion, Horse), 1930
46. Phantasmagoria, 1930
47. Portrait of Mr. Emilio Terry (unfinished), 1930
48. Premature Ossification of a Railroad Station, 1930
49. The Average Bureaucrat, 1930
50. The Bleeding Roses, 1930
51. The Feeling of Becoming, 1930
52. The Font, 1930
53. The Great Masturbator, 1930
54. The Hand, 1930

55. William Tell, 1930
56. Board of Demented Associations (Fireworks), 1931
57. Combinations (or The Combined Dalínian Phantasms; Ants, Keys, Nails), 1931
58. Gradiva, 1931
59. Gradiva Finds the Anthropomorphic Ruins, 1931
60. Landscape, 1931
61. Loneliness, 1931
62. Mme. Reese, 1931
63. On the Seashore, 1931
64. Partial Hallucination: Six Apparitions of Lenin on a Piano, 1931
65. Plant transformation, 1931
66. Portrait of Gala, 1931
67. Remorse, or Sphinx Embedded in the Sand, 1931
68. Scatalogical Object Functioning Symbolically (The Surrealist Shoe), 1931
69. Shades of Night Descending, 1931
70. Symbiosis Between the Head and Shell, 1931
71. The Dream, 1931
72. The Old Age of William Tell, 1931
73. The Persistence of Memory, 1931
74. The Sense of Speed, 1931
75. They Were There, 1931
76. Untided (William Tell and Gradiva), 1931
77. Woman Sleeping in a Landscape, 1931
78. The Spectre and the Phantom, 1931
79. The Dream Approaches, 1931
80. Agnostic Symbol, 1932
81. Angelus, 1932
82. Anthropomorphic Bread, 1932
83. Anthropomorphic Bread, 1932
84. Automatic Beginning of a Portrait of Gala (unfinished), 1932

**85.** Babaouo - Publicity Announcement for the Publication of the Scenario of the Film, 1932
**86.** Diurnal Fantasies, 1932
**87.** Eggs on Plate without the Flat, 1932
**88.** Fried Egg on the Plate without the Plate, 1932
**89.** Galatea of the Spheres, 1932
**90.** Glow of Laport, 1932
**91.** Memory of the Child Woman, 1932
**92.** Memory of the Child-Woman, 1932
**93.** Nostalgia of the Cannibal, 1932
**94.** Paranoic Metamorphosis of Gala's Face, 1932
**95.** Phosphene of Laporte, 1932
**96.** Surrealist Architecture, 1932
**97.** Surrealist Essay, 1932
**98.** Surrealist Object Gauge of Instantaneous Memory, 1932
**99.** The Birth of Liquid Desires, 1932
**100.** The Birth of Liquid Fears, 1932
**101.** The Invisible Harp, Fine and Medium./Harpe invisible fine et moyenne, 1932
**102.** The Invisible Man, 1932
**103.** The Knight at the Tower, 1932
**104.** The Meeting of the Illusion and the Arrested Moment - Fried Eggs Presented in a Spoon, 1932
**105.** The True Painting of the "Isle of the Dead" by Arnold Böcklin at the Hour of the Angelus, 1932
**106.** The Veiled Heart, 1932
**107.** Untitled - Female Figure with Catalonian Bread, 1932
**108.** Ordinary French Loaf with Two Fried Eggs, 1932
**109.** Ambivalent Image, 1933
**110.** Gala and The Angelus of Millet Before the Imminent Arrival of the Conical Anamorphoses, 1933
**111.** Geological evolution, 1933

112. Myself at the Age of Ten When I Was the Grasshopper Child, 1933
113. Necrophiliac Fountain Flowing from a Grand Piano, 1933
114. Portrait of Gala, 1933
115. Portrait of Gala with Two Lamb Chops Balanced on Her Shoulder, 1933
116. Retrospective Bust of a Woman, 1933
117. Sugar Sphinx, 1933
118. The Architectonic Angelus of Millet, 1933
119. The Enigma of William Tell, 1933
120. The Invisible Man, 1933
121. The Phantom Cart, 1933
122. The Phantom Wagon, 1933
123. The Phenomenon of Ecstasy, 1933
124. The Triangular Hour, 1933
125. Untitled - Death Outside the Head - Paul Eluard, 1933
126. Aerodynamic Chair, 1934
127. Allegory of an American Christmas, 1934
128. Apparition of My Cousin Carolinetta on the Beach at Rosas, 1934
129. Atavism at Twilight, 1934
130. Atavistic Vestiges After the Rain, 1934
131. Atmospheric Skull Sodomizing a Grand Piano, 1934
132. Barber Saddened by the Persistence of Good Weather (The Anguished Barber), 1934
133. Cannibalism of the Praying Mantis of Lautreamont, 1934
134. Cardinal, Cardinal, 1934
135. Dreams on a Beach, 1934
136. Eclipse and Vegetable Osmosis, 1934
137. Enigmatic Elements in the Landscape, 1934
138. Figure and Drapery in a Landscape, 1934
139. Figure with Drawers for a Four-part Screen, 1934

140. Ghost of Vermeer Van Delft, 1934

141. Illustration to the 'Songs of Maldoror' Isidore Ducasse, Count Lautréamont, 1934

142. Javanese Mannequin, 1934

143. Landscape with Mysterious Details, 1934

144. Masochistic Instrument, 1934

145. Meditation on the Harp, 1934

146. Melancholy - to Marcel Remy in Friendship, 1934

147. Moment de Transition, 1934

148. Morning Ossification of the Cypress, 1934

149. Night Spectre on the Beach, 1934

150. Paranoiac-Astral Image, 1934

151. Persistence of Fair Weather, 1934

152. Portrait of Gala with a Lobster (Portrait of Gala with Aeroplane Nose), 1934

153. Sad Barber of Good Times Cruelty, 1934

154. Skull with its Lyric Appendage Leaning on a Bedside Table which should have the Exact Temperature of a Cardinal's Nest, 1934

155. Surrealist Knight for a Four-part Screen, 1934

156. Surrealist Knights for a Four-part Screen, Centre Right,, 1934

157. Surrealist Poster, 1934

158. Surrealist Warriors for a Four-part Screen, Centre Left, 1934

159. The Ghost of Vermeer Van Delft, 1934

160. The Ghost of Vermeer van Delft which Can Be Used as a Table, 1934

161. The Hour of the Crackled Visage, 1934

162. The Invisible Harp, 1934

163. The Isle of the Dead - Centre, Section, 1934

164. The Knight of Death, 1934

165. The Mysterious Source of Harmony, 1934

166. The Spectre of the Angelus, 1934

167. The Tower, 1934
168. Untitled (Desert Landscape), 1934
169. Untitled (Dreams on the Beach), 1934
170. West Side of the Isle of the Dead, 1934
171. Archeological Reminiscence Millet's Angelus, 1935
172. Exquisite Cadaver, 1935
173. Face of Mae West Which May Be Used as an Apartment, 1935
174. Gangsterism and Goofy Vision of New York, 1935
175. Mediumnistic-Paranoiac Image, 1935
176. Nostalgic Echo, 1935
177. Paranoiac Critical Solitude, 1935
178. Paranoiac Visage, 1935
179. Poster Project, 1935
180. Puzzle of Autumn, 1935
181. Solitude - Anthropomorphic Echo, 1935
182. The Angelus of Gala, 1935
183. The Echo of the Vold, 1935
184. The Horseman of Death, 1935
185. The Ship, 1935
186. The Surrealist Mystery of New York, 1935
187. Woman with a Head of Roses, 1935
188. A Chemist Lifting with Extreme Precaution the Cuticle of a Grand Piano, 1936
189. A Couple with Their Heads Full of Clouds, 1936
190. Ampurdanese Yang and Yin, 1936
191. Animated Surrealist Landscape, 1936
192. Apparition of the Town of Delft, 1936
193. Autumnal Cannibalism, 1936
194. Bread on the Head of the Prodigal Son, 1936
195. City of drawers, 1936
196. Couple with Clouds in Their Heads (Man), 1936
197. Couple with Clouds in Their Heads (Woman), 1936
198. Couple with Their Heads Full of Clouds, 1936

**199.** Cover of 'Minotaure' Magazine, 1936
**200.** Decalcomania, 1936
**201.** Forgotten Horizon, 1936
**202.** Geological justice, 1936
**203.** Head of a woman in the form of a battle, 1936
**204.** Hypnagogic Monument, 1936
**205.** Landscape with Girl Skipping Rope, 1936
**206.** Man with His Head Full of Clouds, 1936
**207.** Morphological Echo, 1936
**208.** Morphological Echo', 1936
**209.** Necrophiliac Springtime, 1936
**210.** Night and Day Clothes of the Body, 1936
**211.** Paranonia, 1936
**212.** Premonition of Civil War, 1936
**213.** Soft Construction with Boiled Beans: Premonition of Civil War, 1936
**214.** Suburbs of a Paranoiac Critical Town, Afternoon on the Outskirts of European History, 1936
**215.** Sun Table, 1936
**216.** Surrealist Composition with Invisible Figures, 1936
**217.** The Chemist of Ampurden in Search of Absolutely Nothing, 1936 (oil on panel), 1936
**218.** The Great Paranoiac, 1936
**219.** The Man with the Head of Blue Hortensias, 1936
**220.** The Sign of Anguish, 1936
**221.** Two Figures, 1936
**222.** Venus de Milo with Drawers, 1936
**223.** Venus de Milo with Drawers, 1936
**224.** White Calm, 1936
**225.** Woman with Drawers, 1936
**226.** Singularities, 1936
**227.** Three Women with Heads of Flowers Finding the Skin of A, 1936
**228.** Anatomical Studies - Transfer Series, 1937

**229.** Ant Face, 1937
**230.** Average Pagan Landscape, 1937
**231.** Cannibalism of the Objects, 1937
**232.** Swans Reflecting Elephants, 1937
**233.** Enchanted Beach (Long, Siphon), 1937
**234.** Herodias, 1937
**235.** Invention of the Monsters, 1937
**236.** Knights of Death, 1937
**237.** Mae West Lips Sofa, 1937
**238.** Perspectives, 1937
**239.** Queen Salome, 1937
**240.** The Metamorphosis of Narcissus, 1937
**241.** Woman with Flower Head, 1937
**242.** Flaming Giraffe, 1937
**243.** Apparition of Face and Fruit Dish on a Beach, 1938
**244.** Debris of an Automobile Giving Birth to a Blind Horse Biting a Telephone, 1938
**245.** Enchanted Beach with Three Fluid Graces, 1938
**246.** Imperial Violets, 1938
**247.** Impression of Africa, 1938
**248.** Invisible Afghan with the Apparition on the Beach of the Face of Garcia Lorca in the Form of a Fruit Dish with Three Figs, 1938
**249.** Landscape with Telephones on a Plate, 1938
**250.** Lobster Telephone, 1938
**251.** Lobster Telephone, 1938
**252.** Mountain Lake, 1938
**253.** Drawing For "Bacchanale": Ludwig II Of Bavaria, 1938
**254.** Palladio's Corridor of Dramatic Surprise, 1938
**255.** Palladio's Thalia Corridoe, 1938
**256.** Spain, 1938
**257.** The Alert, 1938
**258.** The Endless Enigma, 1938

**259.** The Enigma of Hitler, 1938
**260.** The Sublime Moment, 1938
**261.** The Transparent Simulacrum of the Feigned Image, 1938
**262.** The Enchanted Beach, 1938
**263.** Actress Betty Stockfeld Is Metamorphosed into a Nurse, 1939
**264.** Baby Map of the World, 1939
**265.** Ballerina in a Death's Head, 1939
**266.** Bulgarian Child Eating a Rat, 1939
**267.** Mad Tristan, 1939
**268.** Metamorphosis of the Five Allegories of Giovanni Bellini, 1939
**269.** Philosopher Illuminated by the Light of the Moon and the Setting Sun, 1939
**270.** Psychoanalysis and Morphology Meet, 1939
**271.** Set for 'Bacchanale', 1939
**272.** Shirley Temple, 1939
**273.** The Dream of Venus, 1939
**274.** Untitled - Figure (unfinished), 1939
**275.** Group of Women Imitating the Gestures of a Schooner, 1940
**276.** March of Time Comittee - Papillon, 1940
**277.** Slave Market with the Disappearing Bust of Voltaire, 1940
**278.** Spider Of The Evening, 1940
**279.** Two Pieces of Bread Expressing the Sentiment of Love, 1940
**280.** Book Transforming Itself into a Nude Woman, 1940
**281.** Corrosive, 1940
**282.** The Three Ages, 1940
**283.** Allegory of Sunset Air (Allegory of the Everning), 1941
**284.** Car Clothing (Clothed Automobile), 1941
**285.** Costume for a Nude with a Codfish Tail, 1941

286. Design for Set Curtain for Labyrinth I, 1941
287. Invisible Bust of Voltaire, 1941
288. Labyrinth II, 1941
289. Mysterious Mouth Appearing in the Back of My Nurse, 1941
290. Honey is Sweeter than Blood, 1941
291. Original Sin, 1941
292. Portrait of Gala, 1941
293. Portrait of Mrs. George Tait, II, 1941
294. Ruin with Head of Medusa and Landscape, 1941
295. Soft Self-Portrait with Fried Bacon, 1941
296. Temple - Sketch for a Set Design, 1941
297. The Face of War, 1941, Wikipedia article
298. The Golden Age - Family of Marsupial Centaurs, 1941
299. The Triumph of Nautilus, 1941
300. Birth of a New World, 1942
301. Decor for 'Romeo et Juliet', 1942
302. Design for the set of 'Romeo and Juliet' (backdrops and wing flats), 1942
303. Equestrian Parade (possibly Set Design for 'Romeo and Juliet'), 1942
304. Juliet's Tomb, 1942
305. Melancholy, 1942
306. Mural Painting for Helena Rubinstein (panel 1), 1942
307. Mural Painting for Helena Rubinstein (panel 2), 1942
308. Mural Painting for Helena Rubinstein (panel 3), 1942
309. Nude on the Plain of Rosas, 1942
310. Portrait of Mrs. Luther Greene, 1942
311. Portrait of Mrs. Ortiz-Linares, 1942
312. Portrait of the Marquis De Cuevas, 1942
313. Romeo and Juliet Memorial, 1942
314. Saint George and the Dragon, 1942
315. Sheep, 1942
316. Study for the set of 'Romeo and Juliet', 1942

317. The Flames, They Call, 1942
318. Two Harlequins, 1942
319. Untitled - for the campaign against venereal disease, 1942
320. Untitled - Set Design (Figures Cut in Three), 1942
321. Reclining girl in sheep, 1942
322. Geopolitical Child Watching the Birth of the New Man, 1943
323. Madonna, 1943
324. Painting for the backdrop of 'Cafe De Chinitas', 1943
325. Portrait of Ambassador Cardenas, 1943
326. Portrait of Mrs. Harrison Williams, 1943
327. Princess Arthchil Gourielli (Helena Rubinstein), 1943
328. Stage Curtain for the Ballet 'Cafe De Chinitas', 1943
329. The Poetry of America (unfinished), 1943
330. The Triumph of Tourbillon, 1943
331. Dance, 1944
332. Dream Caused by the Flight of a Bee around a Pomegranate a Second before Awakening, 1944, Wikipedia article
333. Music - The Red Orchestra, 1944
334. Paranoia (Surrealist Figures), 1944
335. Study for Sentimental Colloquy, 1944
336. Study for the Backdrop of 'Mad Tristan' (Act II), 1944
337. Study for the Set of the Ballet 'Tristan Insane', 1944
338. Tristan and Isolde, 1944
339. Untitled - Design for the ball in the dream sequence in 'Spellbound', 1944
340. Untitled - The Seven Arts, 1944
341. Untitled -The Seven Arts, 1944
342. Autumn Sonata, 1945
343. Design for the Film 'Spellbound' (1), 1945
344. Design for the Film 'Spellbound' (2), 1945
345. Design for the set of the film 'Spellbound', 1945

**346.** Don Quixote and the Windmills, 1945

**347.** Fountain of Milk Spreading Itself Uselessly on Three Shoes, 1945

**348.** My Wife, Nude, Contemplating Her Own Flesh Becoming Stairs, Three Vertebrae of a Column, Sky and Architecture, 1945

**349.** Portrait of Frau. Isabel Styler-Tas, 1945

**350.** Resurrection of the Flesh, 1945

**351.** Spellbound, 1945

**352.** The Broken Bridge and the Dream, 1945

**353.** The Eye, 1945

**354.** Three Apparitions of the Visage of Gala, 1945

**355.** Untitled - Portrait of a Woman, 1945

**356.** Untitled - Scene with Marine Allegory, 1945

**357.** Victory (Woman Metamorphosing Into A Boat With Angels), 1945

**358.** Melancholy Atomic, 1945

**359.** Apparition of a Couple in the Desert, 1946

**360.** Apparition of a Woman and Suspended Architecture in the Desert, 1946

**361.** Christmas (Noel), 1946

**362.** Composition - Portrait of Mrs. Eva Kolsman, 1946

**363.** Double Image for 'Destino', 1946

**364.** Flower in the Desert, 1946

**365.** Giant Flying Mocca Cup with an Inexplicable Five Metre Appendage, 1946

**366.** Nude in the Desert Landscape, 1946

**367.** The Stain, 1946

**368.** The Temptation of St. Anthony, 1946

**369.** Untitled (Spanish Dances in a Landscape), 1946

**370.** Dematerialization Near the Nose of Nero, 1947

**371.** Design for 'Destino', 1947

**372.** Design for 'Destino', 1947

373. Feather Equilibrium (Interatomic Balance of a Swans Feather), 1947
374. Portrait of Picasso, 1947
375. Rock and Infuriated Horse Sleeping Under the Sea, 1947
376. Three Sphinxes of Bikini, 1947
377. Lada Atomica (first unfinished version), 1948
378. Portrait of Mrs. Mary Sigall, 1948
379. Portrait of Nada Pachevich, 1948
380. Study for a Portrait (unfinished), 1948
381. The Elephants (Large), 1948
382. Untitled (Landscape), 1948
383. Four Armchairs in the Sky, 1949
384. La Turbie' - Sir James Dunn Seated, 1949
385. Lada Atomica, 1949
386. Set Design for the Ballet 'Los Sacos Del Molinero', 1949
387. Set design for the ballet 'Los Sacos Del Molinero', 1949
388. Set design for the ballet 'Los Sacos Del Molinero', 1949
389. Set design for the ballet 'Los Sacos Del Molinero', 1949
390. The First Study for the Madonna of Port Lligat, 1949
391. Backdrop for 'Don Juan Tenorio', 1950
392. Christ in Perspective, 1950
393. Cork (study for 'The Madonna of Port Lligat'), 1950
394. Dalí at the Age of Six When He Thought He Was a Girl Lifting the Skin of the Water to See the Dog Sleeping in the Shade of the Sea, 1950
395. Dalí's Moustache, 1950
396. Erotic Beach, 1950
397. Gala as Madonna of Port Lligat, 1950
398. Landscape of Port Lligat, 1950
399. Study for a Backdrop, 1950
400. The Madonna of Port Lligat, 1950
401. Celestial Coronation, 1951

**402.** Christ of St. John of the Cross, 1951
**403.** Explosive Madonna, 1951
**404.** Landscape with Cavalier and Gala, 1951
**405.** Mystical Carnation, 1951
**406.** Portrait of a Child (unfinished), 1951
**407.** Portrait of Colonel Jack Warner, 1951
**408.** Portrait of Katharina Cornell, 1951
**409.** Portrait of Mrs Jack Warner, 1951
**410.** Raphaelesque Head Exploding, 1951
**411.** Study for 'Christ of St. John of the Cross', 1951
**412.** The Queen of the Butterflies, 1951
**413.** The Wheelbarrow (Pantheon Formed by Twisted Wheelbarrows), 1951
**414.** Women forming a skull, 1951
**415.** Arithmosophic Cross, 1952
**416.** Assumpta Corpuscularia Lapislazulina, 1952
**417.** Corpuscular Madonna, 1952
**418.** Eucharistic Still Life, 1952
**419.** Madonna in Particles, 1952
**420.** Nuclear Cross, 1952
**421.** Opposition, 1952
**422.** The Angel of Port Lligat, 1952
**423.** The Angel of Port Lligat, 1952
**424.** Transparent Horse, 1952
**425.** The Royal Heart, 1953
**426.** Crucifixion, 1954
**427.** Crucifixion (Corpus Hypercubicus), 1954
**428.** Equestrian Fantasy Portrait of Lady Dunn, 1954
**429.** Galatée, 1954
**430.** Head Bombarded with Grains of Wheat (Particle Head Over the Village of Cadaques), 1954
**431.** Melting Watch, 1954
**432.** Microphysical Madonna, 1954
**433.** Portrait of Gala with Rhinocerotic Symptoms, 1954

434. Portrait of Mrs. Ann Woodward, 1954
435. Portrait of Mrs. Reeves, 1954
436. Rhinocerotic Figure of Phidias' Illisos, 1954
437. Statue of Olympic Zeus, 1954
438. The Colossus of Rhodes, 1954
439. The Lighthouse at Alexandria, 1954
440. The Lighthouse at Alexandria, 1954
441. The Maximum Speed of Raphael's Madonna, 1954
442. Two Adolescents, 1954
443. Young Virgin Auto-Sodomized by the Horns of Her Own Chastity, 1954
444. Dalí Nude, in Contemplation Before the Five Regular Bodies, 1954
445. The Disintegration of the Persistence of Memory, 1954
446. Ascensionist Saint Cecilia, 1955
447. Blue Horns. Design for a Scarf, 1955
448. Dalí Combat, 1955
449. Portrait of Laurence Olivier in the Role of Richard III, 1955
450. Rhinocerotic Figures, 1955
451. Rhinocerotic Portrait of Vermeer's 'Lacemaker', 1955
452. The Paranoiac-Critical Study of Vermeer's Lacemaker, 1955
453. The Sacrament of the Last Supper, 1955
454. Anti-Protonic Assumption, 1956
455. Assumpta Canaveral, 1956
456. Fancy Costumes, 1956
457. Living Still Life, 1956
458. Rhinocerotic Gooseflesh, 1956
459. Saint Surrounded by Three Pi-Mesons, 1956
460. Skull of Zurbaran, 1956
461. St. Helena of Port Lligat, 1956
462. Study for a fruit bowl in 'Still Life - Fast Moving', 1956
463. The Infant Jesus, 1956

**464.** The Motionless Swallow. Study for 'Still Life - Fast Moving', 1956

**465.** Untitled (Landscape with Butterflies), 1956

**466.** Butterfly Landscape (The Great Masturbator in a Surrealist Landscape with D.N.A.), 1957

**467.** Celestial Ride, 1957

**468.** Metamorphosed Women, 1957

**469.** Modern Rhapsody, 1957

**470.** Music - The Red Orchestra, 1957

**471.** Rock 'n Roll, 1957

**472.** Santiago El Grande, 1957

**473.** Sorcery, 1957

**474.** Swallow, 1957

**475.** The Duke of Urbino (Portrait of Count Theo Rossi Di Montelera), 1957

**476.** The Grand Opera, 1957

**477.** Untitled (Surrealist Landscape), 1957

**478.** Ascension, 1958

**479.** Christ. From 'The Apocalypse of St. John', 1958

**480.** Clown for 'The Amazing Adventure of the Lacemaker and the Rhinoceros', 1958

**481.** Cosmic Madonna, 1958

**482.** Dionysus Spitting the Complete Image of Cadaques on the Tip of the Tongue of a Three-Storied Gaudinian Woman, 1958

**483.** Landscape Near Port Lligat, 1958

**484.** Meditative Rose, 1958

**485.** Metamorphosis of Hitler's Face into a Moonlit Landscape with Accompaniment, 1958

**486.** Portrait of Sir James Dunn, 1958

**487.** Religious Scene in Particles, 1958

**488.** The Sistine Madonna, 1958

**489.** Velázquez Painting the Infanta Margarita with the Lights and Shadows of His Own Glory, 1958

490. Port Lligat at Sunset, 1959
491. Portrait of Reinaldo Herrera Marquis De Torre Casa, 1959
492. The Discovery of America by Christopher Columbus, 1959
493. The Virgin of Guadalupe, 1959
494. Woman Undressing, 1959
495. A Propos of the 'Treatise on Cubic Form' by Juan de Herrera, 1960
496. Birth of a Divinity, 1960
497. Chair with the Wings of a Vulture, 1960
498. Goddess Leaning on Her Elbow - Continuum of the Four Buttocks or Five Rhinoceros Horns Making a Virgin or Birth of a Deity, 1960
499. Hyperxiological Sky, 1960
500. Portrait of Countess Ghislaine d'Oultremont, 1960
501. Portrait of Juan de Pareja Adjusting a String on His Mandolin, 1960
502. Portrait of Mrs. Fagen, 1960
503. Portrait of St. Jerome, 1960
504. San Salvador and Antonio Gaudi Fighting for the Crown of the Virgin, 1960
505. The Cosmic Athlete, 1960
506. The Ecumenical Council, 1960
507. The Ecumenical Council, 1960
508. The Life of Mary Magdalene, 1960
509. The Maids-in-Waiting (Las Meninas), 1960
510. Untitled, 1960
511. Untitled (The Lady of Avignon), 1960
512. The Trinity, 1960
513. Portrait of Juan de Pareja Repairing a String of His Mandolin, 1960
514. St. Peter's in Rome, 1960
515. Mohammed's Dream (Homage to Fortuny), 1961

**516.** Battle of Tétouan, 1962

**517.** Macrophotographic Self-Portrait with the Appearance of Gala, 1962

**518.** Portrait of Mr. Fagen, 1962

**519.** St. George and the Dragon, 1962

**520.** The Alchemist, 1962

**521.** The Sacred Heart of Jesus, 1962

**522.** Twist in the Studio of Velazquez, 1962

**523.** Vision of Fatima, 1962

**524.** Fifty Abstract Paintings Which as Seen from Two Yards Change into Three Lenins Masquerading as Chinese and as Seen from Six Yards Appear as the Head of a Royal Bengal Tiger, 1963

**525.** Galacidalacidesoxyribonucleicacid, 1963

**526.** Hercules Lifts the Skin of the Sea and Stops Venus for an Instant from Waking Love, 1963

**527.** Portrait of My Dead Brother, 1963

**528.** Study for Deoxyribonucleic Acid Arabs, 1963

**529.** Study for Deoxyribonucleic Acid Arabs, 1963

**530.** The Madonna and the Mystical Rose, 1963

**531.** Untitled (Still Life with Lilies), 1963

**532.** Landscape with Flies, 1964

**533.** Untitled (St. John), 1964

**534.** The Simoniacs, 1964

**535.** Crucifixion (Dedication; For Gala Queen of the Divine DalH), 1965

**536.** Laocoon Tormented by Flies, 1965

**537.** Moth and Flame. Candelstick, 1965

**538.** Portrait of Gala (Gala Against the Light), 1965

**539.** Portrait of Mrs. Ruth Daponte, 1965

**540.** Salvador Dalí in the Act of Painting Gala in the Apotheosis of the Dollar, 1965

**541.** The Railway Station at Perpignan, 1965

**542.** The Sun of Dalí, 1965

**543.** Untitled (St. John from Behind), 1965
**544.** Moses and the Pharaoh, 1966
**545.** Tuna Fishing, 1967
**546.** Tuna Fishing (advanced State), 1967
**547.** David et Philistaeus (1 Samuel 17:43), 1967
**548.** Omnes de Saba venient, 1967
**549.** The Mountains of Cape Creus on the March, 1967
**550.** Fisherman of Port Lligat Mending His Net, 1968
**551.** Mad Mad Mad Minerva - Illustration for 'Memories of Surrealism', 1968
**552.** Tauromachia I - The Torero, the Kill (third and final round of the bullfight), 1968
**553.** Hour of the Monarchy, 1969
**554.** The Pool of Tears, 1969
**555.** Untitled (Still Life with White Cloth), 1969
**556.** Untitled (Surrealist Angel), 1969
**557.** The Hallucinogenic Toreador, 1970
**558.** Nude Figures at Cape Creus, 1970
**559.** Portrait of John Theodoracopoulos, 1970
**560.** Roger Freeing Angelica (St. George and the Damsel), 1970
**561.** Study for the Decoration of the Ceiling in Pubol, 1970
**562.** Untitled (Michelangelo Head with Drawers), 1970
**563.** Hannibal crossing the Aps, 1970
**564.** Caligula's Horse (Dalí's Horses), 1971
**565.** Ceiling of the Hall of Gala's Chateau at Pubol, 1971
**566.** Figure with Flag. Illustration for 'Memories of Surrealism', 1971
**567.** The Second Coming of Christ, 1971
**568.** Gala's Dream (Dream of Paradise), 1972
**569.** Marilyn Monroe, 1972
**570.** Overture in Trompe l'Oeil, 1972

**571.** Polyhedron. Basketball Players Being Transformed into Angels (Assembling a Hologram - the Central Element), 1972

**572.** Self-Portrait (Photomontage with the famous 'Mao-Marilyn' that Philippe Halsman created at Dalí's wish), 1972

**573.** Space Eve, 1972

**574.** The Daughter of the West Wind, 1972

**575.** Untitled (Stereoscopic Painting), 1972

**576.** Dalí from the Back Painting Gala from the Back Eternalized by Six Virtual Corneas Provisionally Reflected in Six Real Mirrors, 1973

**577.** First Cylindric Crono-Hologram. Portrait of Alice Cooper's Brain, 1973

**578.** Gala's Castle at Pubol, 1973

**579.** Hitler Masturbating, 1973

**580.** Las Galas of Port Lligat, 1973

**581.** Palace of the Winds, 1973

**582.** Portrait of Dr. Brian Mercer, 1973

**583.** The Sleeping Smoker, 1973

**584.** The Way to Pubol, 1973

**585.** Homage To Duchamp, 1973

**586.** Armchair with Landscape Painted for Gala's Chateau at Pubol, 1974

**587.** Battle in the Clouds, 1974

**588.** Cranach Metamorphosis (Woman in a Mirror), 1974

**589.** Equestrian Portrait of Carmen Bordiu-Franco, 1974

**590.** The Palace of the Wind, 1974

**591.** The Palace of the Wind, 1974

**592.** To Meli, 1974

**593.** Transformation of 'Antiques' Magazine Cover into the Apparition of a Face, 1974

**594.** Wounded Soft Watch, 1974

**595.** Gala Contemplating the Mediterranean Sea Which at Twenty Meters Becomes the Portrait of Abraham Lincoln - Homage to Rothko (first version), 1975

**596.** Homage to Raimundus Lullus (design for a ceiling painting), 1975

**597.** The Chair, 1975

**598.** The Chair (stereoscopic work, right component), 1975

**599.** The Whole Dalí in a Face, 1975

**600.** Gala Contemplating the Mediterranean Sea Which at Eighteen Metres Becomes the Portrait of Abraham Lincoln, 1976

**601.** Soft Monster (Monstruo blando adormercido), 1976

**602.** The Chair, 1976

**603.** The Wash Basin, 1976

**604.** Angelic Landscape, 1977

**605.** Dalí Lifting the Skin of the Mediterranean Sea to Show Gala the Birth of Venus, 1977

**606.** Dalí's Hand Drawing Back the Golden Fleece in the Form of a Cloud to Show Gala,Completely Nude,the Dawn,Very,Very Far Away Behind the Sun, 1977

**607.** Fertility, 1977

**608.** Las Meninas (The Maids-in-Waiting), 1977

**609.** Nike, Victory Goddess of Samothrace, Appears in a Tree Bathed in Light, 1977

**610.** Portrait of Gala, 1977

**611.** Surrealist Angel, 1977

**612.** Triomphe De L'Amour, 1977

**613.** Allegory of Spring, 1978

**614.** Ampurdanese Landscape,, 1978

**615.** Cybernetic ODalísque, 1978

**616.** Cybernetic ODalísuqe-Homage to Bela Julesz, 1978

**617.** Dark Tapeworms, 1978

**618.** Gala's Christ, 1978

**619.** Landscape Near Ampurdan, 1978

**620.** The Eye of the Angelus, 1978
**621.** The Harmony of the Spheres, 1978
**622.** Woman with Egg and Arrows, 1978
**623.** Copy of a Rubens Copy of a Leonardo, 1979
**624.** Dawn, Noon, Sunset and Dusk, 1979
**625.** Long Live the Station at Perpignan, Long Live Figueras, 1979
**626.** Nude and Horse with Metamorphosis (unfinished), 1979
**627.** Pentagonal Sardana, 1979
**628.** Pentagonal Sardana, 1979
**629.** Raphaelesque Hallucination, 1979
**630.** Searching for the Fourth Dimension, 1979
**631.** Study for 'Compianto Diabele' by Canova (unfinished), 1979
**632.** The Prince of Sleep (El principe de ensueno), 1979
**633.** Athens Is Burning! The School of Athens and the Fire in the Borgo, 1980
**634.** Athens Is Burning! The School of Athens and the Fire in the Borgo, 1980
**635.** Sleeping Young Narcissus, 1980
**636.** The Cheerful Horse, 1980
**637.** Untitled (Bridge with Reflections; sketch for a dual image picture, unfinished), 1980
**638.** Amphitrite, 1981
**639.** Apparition of the Visage of Aphrodite of Cnidos in a Landscape, 1981
**640.** Argus, 1981
**641.** Gala in a Patio Watching the Sky, Where the Equestrian Figure of Prince Baltasar Carlos and Several Constellations (All) Appear, after Velazquez, 1981
**642.** Great Tapeworm Masturbator, Appears Behind Arcades, 1981

**643.** Group Surrounding a Reclining Nude - Velazquez, 1981
**644.** Hermes, 1981
**645.** Jason Carrying the Golden Fleece (unfinished), 1981
**646.** Landscape, 1981
**647.** Mercury and Argus, 1981
**648.** Ready-to-wear Fashion for Next Spring; 'Garlands, Nests and Flowers', 1981
**649.** Seated Figure Contemplating a 'Great Tapeworm Masturbator', 1981
**650.** Spanish Nobleman with a Cross of Brabant on His Jerkin, 1981
**651.** The Garden of Hours, 1981
**652.** The Path of Enigma, 1981
**653.** The Path of Enigmas (first version), 1981
**654.** The Path of Enigmas (second version), 1981
**655.** The Pearl, 1981
**656.** The Tower of Enigmas, 1981
**657.** The Towers, 1981
**658.** Tower, 1981
**659.** Tower, 1981
**660.** Untitled (Female Bust with Draped Cloth), 1981
**661.** Untitled (Skin of a Beach), 1981
**662.** After Michelangelo's 'Moses', on the Tomb of Julius II in Rome, 1982
**663.** After the Head of 'Giuliano di Medici, 1982
**664.** Architectural Contortion of El Escorial, 1982
**665.** Atmospherocephalic Figures, 1982
**666.** Classic Figure and Head (unfinished), 1982
**667.** Double Victory of Gaudi, 1982
**668.** El Escorial and Catastrophe-Form Calligraphy, 1982
**669.** Enigma (unfinished version of 'The Three Glorious Enigmas of Gala'), 1982
**670.** Exploded Head, 1982

**671.** Figure in the Water - After a Drawing by Michelangelo for the 'Resurrection of Christ', 1982

**672.** Figure Inspired by the Adam of the Ceiling of the Sistine Chapel, 1982

**673.** Head, after Michelangelo's, 'Giuliano di Medici', 1982

**674.** Mirror Women - Mirror Head, 1982

**675.** Ole, 1982

**676.** Othello Dreaming Venice, 1982

**677.** Pieta, 1982

**678.** Rock Figure after the Head of Christ in the 'Pieta' of Palestrina by Michelangelo, 1982

**679.** Saint Sebastian, 1982

**680.** Sebastian de Morra with Catastrophic Signs, 1982

**681.** Study for 'Ole' (unfinished), 1982

**682.** The Infanta Margarita of Velazquez Appearing in the Silhouette of Horsemen in the Courtyard of the Escorial, 1982

**683.** The Martyr, 1982

**684.** The Three Glorious Enigmas of Gala, 1982

**685.** The Three Glorious Enigmas of Gala(second version), 1982

**686.** Topological Study for 'Exploded Head', 1982

**687.** Untitled - Equestrian Figure of Prince Baltasar Carlos, after Velazquez, with Figures in the Courtyard of the Escorial, 1982

**688.** Untitled (Composition - Courtyard of the Escorial with Figure and Sebastian De Morra, Veldzquez's Dwarf), 1982

**689.** Velazquez Dying Behind the Window on the Left Side Out of Which a Spoon Projects, 1982

**690.** Warrior, 1982

**691.** Bed and Bedside Table Ferociously Attacking a Cello, 1983

**692.** Bed and Two Bedside Tables Ferociously Attacking a Cello, 1983

**693.** Bed and Two Bedside Tables Ferociously Attacking a Cello, 1983

**694.** Bed and Two Bedside Tables Ferociously Attacking a Cello (Final Stage), 1983

**695.** Bed, Chair and Bedside Table Ferociously Attacking a Cello, 1983

**696.** Cutlet and Match - The Chinese Crab, 1983

**697.** St. George Overpowering a Cello, 1983

**698.** The Swallow's Tail, 1983

**699.** Topological Abduction of Europe - Homage to Rene Thom, 1983

**700.** Topological Contortion of a Female Figure, 1983

**701.** Topological Contortion of a Female Figure Becoming a Violoncello, 1983

**702.** Untitled - Head of a Spanish Nobleman, Fashioned by the Catastrophe Model from a Swallow's Tail and Two Halves of a Cello, 1983

**703.** Untitled - Series on Catastrophes, 1983

**704.** Untitled (Figures, Pieta, Catastrophic Signs), 1983

**705.** Warrior Mounted on an Elephant Overpowering a Cello, 1983

**706.** Blue Knot and Ear of Wheat Next to the Castle, *Date Not Specified*

**707.** Cavallo Metafisco, *Date Not Specified*

**708.** Death Knight, *Date Not Specified*

**709.** Female Nude, *Date Not Specified*

**710.** La Tour, *Date Not Specified*

**711.** L'Etoile, *Date Not Specified*

**712.** Pink Knot and Shell on the Seashore, *Date Not Specified*

**713.** Space Elephant, *Date Not Specified*

**714.** Sybyle Agripa, *Date Not Specified*

**715.** The Gold Chalice, *Date Not Specified*

**716.** The Kings Sword, *Date Not Specified*

**717.** The Moon, *Date Not Specified*

For more of Sarah Hobbs Poetry visit:
www.sarahhobbspoetry.co.uk

Or you can purchase more of her publications by visiting:
https://www.amazon.co.uk/Sarah-Hobbs/e/B006L32VS4/

Why not follow Sarah on social media:

- Facebook: http://facebook.com/sarahhobbspoetry
- Twitter: https://twitter.com/hobbspoetry
- YouTube: https://www.youtube.com/channel/UC9syfVJcoaJwREj03m4bt5w
- Instagram: https://www.instagram.com/sarahhobbspoetry/

You can also sign-up to Sarah's monthly email newsletter with updates on her writing and performing by visiting the homepage of her website mentioned above.

*"Dormant goose bumps, beware!*
*This poetry sees beyond the obvious."*
***~ Paul Chimera, Dalí Historian ~***

*"DALÍ: In Verse is more than just an appreciation of Salvador Dali. It is a celebration of his work. Sarah Hobbs captures the emotion and complexity of Dali's paintings, yet her poetry stands alone. DALÍ: In Verse can be enjoyed without knowledge of Dali, but for those that are familiar, it adds another dimension to the artist's work, picking up where he left off."*
***~ Amy Guidry, Contemporary Surrealist Artist ~***

www.ingramcontent.com/pod-product-compliance
Ingram Content Group UK Ltd.
Pitfield, Milton Keynes, MK11 3LW, UK
UKHW041641190726
13854UKWH00006B/2629